Friendship of a Lifetime

written and illustrated by
Emily Williams-Wheeler.

Adventure Publications
Cambridge, Minnesota

Copyright ©1993 by Emily Williams-Wheeler

Published by
Adventure Publications, Inc.
P.O. Box 269
Cambridge, MN 55008

Thank you and love . . . . .
to my dear friend
Cherie

Sept. 25, 1999

From beneath the baubles and lipstick,

between exchanges of laughter and gifts,

and through special secrets shared,

emerges a friendship of a lifetime.

Growing up, the horizon broadens,

new friends share the spotlight —

but sometimes, best friends are enough.

There are light-hearted
times of love – all

and heavy-hearted moments
of love gone.

Milestones are passed,

boundaries are moved,

and the focus of life changes.

But a phone call is all that is needed

to bring one home to the heart.

The little complications

and the toughest decisions

seem easier in the
company of a friend.

By bearing life's great labors together,

the fruits of the labor can be shared.

Meanwhile, it's the little indulgences

that sweeten an already
pleasant afternoon.

Whether it's the view from home,

or the view from abroad,

looking back, looking ahead,
its always a picture of contentment.

For more information
on books by
Emily Williams-Wheeler,
contact your local
gift / book store or
Adventure Publications
1·800·678·7006.